A Guide for Curricular Change

Revising
General Education—
And Avoiding the Potholes

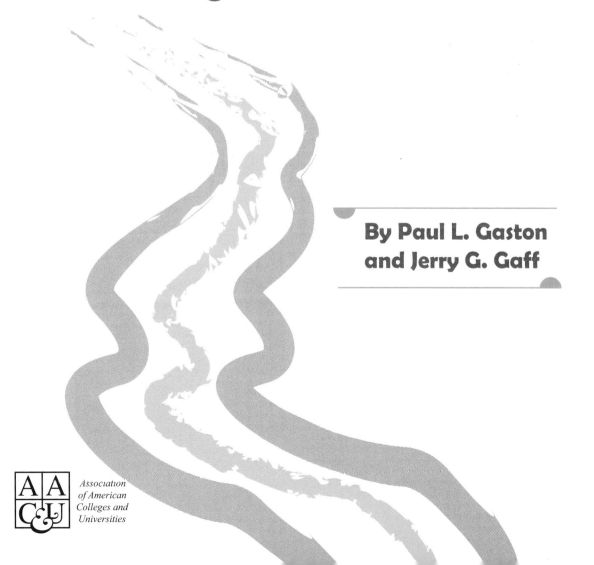

**By Paul L. Gaston
and Jerry G. Gaff**

AAC&U

Association
of American
Colleges and
Universities

1818 R Street, NW, Washington, DC 20009

ISBN: 978-0-9796181-8-5

To order additional copies of this publication or to learn about other AAC&U publications,
visit www.aacu.org, e-mail pub_desk@aacu.org, or call 202.387.3760.

Contents

Introduction

At the end of the 1970s, leaders of American higher education turned their attention to the improvement of undergraduate general education thanks to three signal events: the Carnegie Foundation for the Advancement of Teaching (1977) declared general education "a disaster area"; Ernest Boyer, the U.S. commissioner of education, and his assistant Martin Kaplan (1977) called for a focus on social needs and suggested a common core curriculum as a means to secure nothing less than "survival"; and the Task Force on the Core Curriculum at Harvard College (1978) recommended a core curriculum for students at that influential university. Colleges and universities across the country soon had their faculties discussing improvements in general education—and the conversations continue to this day.

An influential article arising from this era was "Avoiding the Potholes: Strategies for Reforming General Education" (Gaff 1980). It summarized the lessons learned about the process of curricular change by fourteen diverse colleges and universities participating in the Project on General Education Models sponsored by the Society for Values in Higher Education. Over the years, this article has been found useful by faculty members and academic administrators throughout higher education as they have reviewed and strengthened general education curricula.

Since 1991, the Association of American Colleges and Universities (AAC&U) has conducted an annual, weeklong institute for faculty and administrators from campuses seeking to assess and improve the general education of their students. Originally called the Asheville Institute on General Education because of its initial site, the University of North Carolina at Asheville, more recently it has moved among several different campuses. Each institute has invited teams from twenty to thirty institutions, and each team has been provided with copies of books and articles about general education, including "the potholes paper," as it has come to be known. In recent years, the institute staff observed that the article's content was still very relevant but that it needed to be updated. In May 2006 Paul Gaston, a staff member at the institute, volunteered to take the lead in a revision if Jerry Gaff would work with him. Thus began the collaboration that has led to this revised and expanded publication.

The purposes of this new publication are (1) to identify problems, herein called "potholes," often encountered by campus curricular review and revision groups; (2) to describe some ill-fated consequences of seemingly commonsense strategies or procedures adopted by curricular review groups; and (3) to suggest alternative approaches. The purpose is not to provide a ready-made roadmap of the curricular change process, but rather to stimulate thinking among campus leaders so that they can devise the most effective strategies for their own circumstances. And because drivers may sometimes find a brief trip guide useful as a handy supplement to the travelogue, you will find a quick summary of our positive recommendations in appendix A.

The Changing Environment for General Education

By the late 1970s, general education had come to be taken for granted and consisted of a variety of courses in the liberal arts and sciences disciplines so as to provide students with a broad education. But educators were growing concerned that mere breadth was an insufficient requirement for an educated person, and they searched for a more robust view of general education. It soon became clear that it admitted of no single or simple definition. A heuristic definition was offered by the Task Group on General Education (1988, 1) led by the late Joseph Katz: general education is "the knowledge, skills, and attitudes that all of us use and live by during most of our lives—whether as parents, citizens, lovers, travelers, participants in the arts, leaders, volunteers, or good Samaritans." This definition avoided advocacy of any particular content and invited individuals into a conversation to determine the most essential knowledge, skills, and attitudes for students to acquire. Although breadth of knowledge was still important, this definition raised the sights of those who discussed general education. Soon many colleges and universities were hard at work discussing the importance of general education for their students and devising ways to strengthen their current programs.

Even as concerns over undergraduate general education were beginning to claim the public attention, several important paths to reform were beginning to converge. First, increased expectations for institutional accountability, experiments with "performance funding," and concerns regarding institutional identity and competitiveness prompted a growing recognition: general education represents not merely a platform for study in the major, but a critical contributor to and determinant of an institution's overall educational effectiveness. A second path lay in the emerging awareness among employers that individuals presenting the benefits of an effective general education were likely to prove more adaptable to change, more inclined to efficient and cooperative work within groups, more appreciative of diversity, and better prepared to learn on the job (AAC&U 2008, 10–14). As Marvin Suomi, president and CEO of the Kajima Corporation, said at a conference sponsored by Elmhurst College, "today, perhaps more than ever, we need the depth of perspective that a liberal arts education can bring to decision-making, product development, leadership, and other dimensions of business" (Council of Independent Colleges 2003, 12). Finally, increasing competition among colleges and universities for talented students has provided an impetus for promoting strong general education programs as a competitive, marketable advantage. As these paths have come together, many institutions have sought to examine, improve, and assess their general education programs.

Success has hardly been universal, however. For every exemplary program implemented, there have been several institutions that, after weighing ambitious reform plans, have settled for modest, conventional revisions. Why? In many cases, one word will suffice as explanation: "potholes." Hence, one important assumption of this revised essay is that even as the environment for reform has grown more favorable, potholes remain. Indeed, the experience of several decades has shown that those committed to effective reform in general education must take seriously not only the opportunities, but also the challenges that may arise at the various stages leading to implementation.

On the positive side, the road map has become clearer. Largely through the leadership of AAC&U and the Association for Liberal and General Studies, an emerging consensus regarding the essential elements and outcomes of general education can enable those engaged in reform discussions to reach agreement on principles far more quickly than in the past. For example, in 2008, a task force formed at Kent State University to propose a "philosophy of undergraduate education" agreed almost at once that its discussions would be guided by the "Essential Learning Outcomes" described in *College Learning for the New Global Century,* the 2007 report from AAC&U's Liberal Education and America's Promise initiative (see appendix B).

Moreover, the consensus now expresses important recognitions that effectively disarm many once-contentious issues. For instance, few would any longer regard general and professional education as competing interests; strong undergraduate programs align the two and ensure continuity between them. Similarly, there is broad agreement that a curriculum is only as effective as the pedagogy that supports it. Support for active and collaborative approaches, with an emphasis on documented student learning, now informs both general education and the major. And recognition of the importance of diversity, of a global vision, and of examined values has become a point of departure for most discussions of curricular reform.

Another influence on general education reform, one only dimly foreseen in the 1970s, is the dramatic transformation of communications as a result of faster, more capacious computers; software programs that can stimulate, support, and archive discussion; and, of course, the Internet. The advice offered in the original "potholes paper" regarding the importance of frequent communication has assumed a new urgency because of expectations that those engaged with educational reform will connect with all appropriate constituencies persistently, substantively, and creatively, through not just one channel but several.

A further positive change is the now widely shared acknowledgment that students learn most readily by becoming actively involved in their own education (Chen, Gonyea, and Kuh 2008; Astin 1999). With attention both to pedagogical research and to emerging best practices, colleges and universities are increasingly committed to active learning with an important social dimension. Learning communities bring together students with interests in common, often within the precincts of a residence hall, while freshman interest groups offer cohort learning across several related courses. Undergraduate research, supported since 1978 by a national council (now with over nine hundred institutional members), invites undergraduate students, including those in general education science courses, to work closely with faculty members in order to make "an original intellectual or creative contribution to the discipline." And service learning, which the University of Colorado at Boulder defines as a means of relating academic study to work in the community "in ways that enhance both," has moved the educational experience into the community to the advantage of both. Echoing what has become almost a pedagogical commonplace, the University of Colorado statement observes, "we learn best and most deeply by constructing knowledge and rooting it in the immediacies of our personal experience."

And then there is the explosive growth of distance education. Many institutions now offer some of their own general education courses at a distance, and most will accept for transfer credit at least some work provided at a distance by other institutions. How well such courses accomplish their intended purposes remains an important consideration, of course. But for the purposes of this discussion, distance education has become particularly important for placing in high relief such issues as defining and assessing learning outcomes, accommodating different learning styles, and using technology to add value to learning (Potashnik and Capper 1998). Work undertaken within the past five years by the Ohio Learning Network, for instance, has suggested also that strong distance education programs can have a salutary influence on traditional curricula by drawing renewed attention to principles of good practice relevant for all undergraduate education.

Finally, accrediting agencies have determined that institutions must define the student learning goals for general education, assess the achievement of that learning, and use the information obtained through assessment for strengthening the program. While opportune in some ways, this more recent challenge can prove particularly complicated. But it does give impetus to the assessment of specified learning goals across the curriculum as a whole and to the development of intentional ways to cultivate those qualities, largely through a program of general education.

Perhaps the most compelling evidence of positive change in general education reform lies in the success stories of institutions that have effectively distinguished themselves through freshly conceived approaches. At Elon University, for instance, the four-year, fifty-nine-hour General Studies curriculum adds up to a strong institutional "signature." By consciously examining their own values and assumptions in the context of intensive study of the world's cultures, Elon students seek growth in their appreciation for diversity and in their personal capacity for leadership. Similarly, at Portland State University, general education starts with the Freshman Inquiry course. Designed and taught by interdisciplinary teams to learning communities, the course introduces students to the particular challenges and expectations of college-level learning. General education then culminates with a senior-year, multidisciplinary learning community in which students collaborate on research into significant issues facing the Portland community.

The Wagner Plan for the Practical Liberal Arts enables students at Wagner College to pursue a plan of study that integrates liberal studies with in-depth study in the major. Here, too, distinctive program features include intercultural emphases, community engagement, experiential learning, and small-group, collaborative investigation. And at

Miami Dade College, a formal covenant signed in October 2007 commits both the faculty and the student body to a "shared responsibility" for learning outcomes that include analytical skills, critical and creative thinking, cultural knowledge, historical perspectives, social responsibility, technological literacy, aesthetic appreciation, and environmental awareness. Such outcomes, in terms of the covenant, align not only with student success but with the education of "empowered, informed and responsible citizens."

These and many other examples demonstrate the extent to which successful general education reform can, among other things, enhance institutional visibility and competitiveness. Yet, despite these important advances, for a number of reasons, the potholes awaiting those who now seek to strengthen general education have proliferated and, in some instances, grown deeper.

Today's financial challenges both create stresses for general education programs and impose constraints on their reform. When limited funds prompt a decrease in instructional budgets, colleges may be tempted to find savings in general education programs by relying on less costly (and sometimes less fully engaged) part-time and non-tenure-track faculty members. Ross Miller reported in a 2001 AAC&U briefing paper that the percentage of part-time faculty had risen from 34 percent in 1977 to 43 percent in 1998. He observed further that "most part-time faculty, it appears, devote little time to activities generally related to quality in college instruction, i.e. scholarship/research, professional development, etc." By fall 2005, according to a report from the National Center for Education Statistics (Knapp et al. 2007), the percentage of part-time faculty had risen to 47.5 percent. Increased section sizes in general education courses offer another strategy for reducing costs but may inhibit pedagogical innovation. And budget models that assign costs and earnings on a course-by-course or program-by-program basis may discourage interdisciplinary or team-taught courses. Reform initiatives that threaten such cost-saving measures in the interest of improved program quality may prove problematic.

Current curricular realities often reflect such constraints. The fact is that even after more than three decades of determined attention to the opportunities inherent in general education reform, most general education programs continue to operate according to the "distribution" model. Often without much guidance, students choose the required number of hours from specified areas. This approach does not rule out rigorous and coherent programs of study, but it hardly ensures them. Add to the limitations of this model the reality that general education is rarely "owned" by the faculty—in that faculty advancement continues to emphasize specialized research and publication—and it becomes clear why students still report being advised to "get their general education requirements out of the way." The fruits of faculty specialization may be considerable, as Derek Bok has observed in *Our Underachieving Colleges* (2006), but the costs to general education may also be considerable. When a department's most creative and experienced faculty members fail to embody and promote the fruits of a memorable general education, they can undermine even laudable general education goals and frustrate from the start efforts to achieve meaningful reform.

Hence change in general education remains as difficult as ever. Three decades after the launch of this "movement," one might think that much has been learned about the process of curricular change. Yet the professional literature on the topic is remarkably thin. In addition to the original "potholes paper," just a few items stand out. Jack Lindquist's seminal monograph, *Strategies for Change* (1978), was revised and published posthumously in the *Handbook of the Undergraduate Education* (1996) edited by Jerry Gaff and James Ratcliff. And several case studies have analyzed the process of curricular change. Joseph Melusky and Donna Menis (1966) reported the lessons they learned at a small, private, Catholic university; Susan Awbrey (2005) analyzed the change process at a large, public comprehensive university; and Susan Steele (2006) wrote about the same topic at a large, public, research university. But the literature on curricular change remains limited.

Two organizations have developed awards for institutions that demonstrate effective processes of curricular change and effective assessment of student outcomes. The Association for General and Liberal Studies presents awards to institutions that have used exemplary procedures to review and revise their general education programs to cultivate student learning; the two winners in 2008 were the University of North Dakota and Miami Dade College. The Council for Higher Education Accreditation gives awards to institutions that not only articulate student learning goals but present evidence of success, inform the public, and use the results for institutional improvement. The 2009 winners were Northern Arizona University and Delaware Technical and Community College; lessons learned from prior applicants have been summarized by Judith Eaton (2008).

In sum, three decades after general education took center stage in American higher education, it would be gratifying to report that the potholes have been repaired and that the route from curricular review, to proposal development and approval, to implementation and assessment has been made smooth. It would be gratifying—but it would be wrong. The course of curricular change seldom is smooth because the curriculum remains a "battlefield" that engages a number of contending forces. Serious challenges are likely to arise at various stages of the change process, and leaders today—no less than three decades ago—are well advised to study the process of curricular change. They need to develop strategies and procedures that engage their colleagues in a constructive dialogue as they work collaboratively to devise effective general education programs that offer a myriad of advantages to their students and their institutions.

Strategies for Change—and the Potholes They Face

Members of curriculum committees and task forces usually bring much talent and enthusiasm to the task of reviewing, revising, and assessing general education, but few have experience in providing leadership for institutional change. Faculty members tend to be attracted to substantive issues—the nature of general education, the qualities of an educated person, problems with the current program, facets of an ideal general education—and much less interested in the strategies and procedures to be used by the group.

Furthermore, committees and task forces tend to adopt commonsense approaches to fashion a report. Unfortunately, some commonsense approaches turn out to be naive, and those advancing proposals—even good ones—may therefore hit potholes along the way to passage and implementation. Such potholes can slow down the progress of curricular change and, in some cases, lead to a breakdown. Although commonsense approaches sometimes prove to be the best, they are more likely to work if they are consciously chosen in the light of alternatives, rather than seized upon as the only way to proceed.

The biggest pothole to avoid, then, is the notion that strategies to secure approval and implementation of a proposal require attention only when a proposed program has been approved and is about to be implemented. To the contrary, such strategies are critical to the process of curricular review, design, and approval, and they should be considered from the outset. Some committees have learned the hard way that the strategies for curricular change can prove as important as the substance of their proposal, and their experiences may help fellow travelers on the road to general education reform. Many common strategic missteps can be observed in the work of general education task forces and committees. These "potholes" can lead to a rough ride on the road to reform. But we go further than simply erecting hazard indicators. In what follows, we group them into appropriate categories, we suggest different ways of thinking about them, and, where possible, we suggest some detours intended to provide a smoother ride.

What Is the Problem that Needs Fixing?

Sometimes academic leaders underestimate the magnitude of the task of reviewing or assessing general education and devising more effective programs. In reality, thinking through the nature of the undergraduate curriculum is both a large intellectual puzzle and a major political undertaking, in the classic sense that the academic polity must embrace a proposal if it is to become effective. Underestimating the magnitude of the challenge can lead to unrealistic ideas about the duration of the project, the amount of support that may be required, and the usefulness of regular procedures.

A particular complication is that any general education program must be a broadly collective matter. That is, whereas most educational decisions can be made by individuals or small groups of faculty in their departments, the entire faculty must coalesce around a single program of general education. In the words of a report from the Association of American Colleges (1985, 9), the task is "to revive the responsibility of the faculty *as a whole* for the curriculum *as a whole*." This collective effort is as important as it is difficult. Yet there is no challenge in higher education that cannot be made even more difficult. What follows are several ideas that seem reasonable but have, in practice, made significant change in general education *even more formidable* than it needs to be.

Pothole 1: Assume that everyone understands the value of general education and the need for improvement.

During the early years of the AAC&U Institute on General Education, some teams worked enthusiastically to devise ambitious proposals for curricular change. But when they returned home eager to share their best ideas with their colleagues, they discovered that many neither were particularly interested in general education nor thought there was anything wrong with what they were currently doing. Hence, rather than presenting their colleagues with their own plan for change, the team members had first to back up and help their colleagues understand the value and significance of general education, to persuade them there were problems with the current program, and to invite their involvement in making improvements. Since those early days, the institute's curriculum has included an entire track of sessions on the process and politics of curricular change and has encouraged teams to complement their development of specific proposals for curricular change with plans to engage their colleagues in the process of rethinking the general education program.

Pothole 2: Find a program to import.

During the first few years of the Institute on General Education, many of the participating teams arrived in Asheville with the misconception that they would be presented with an array of model programs. They expected to look over a menu, make their selections, and take a proposed program back to their schools for debate and speedy approval. Instead, the institute faculty guided the task force members in developing their own programs. Over time, it became clear to both faculty and institute participants alike that a program for strengthening general education must be designed to embody each institution's character, the needs of its students, and the strengths and interests of its faculty. As noted above, through thoughtfully conceived general education programs, colleges and universities not only can enhance the education of their students, but also have the opportunity to differentiate themselves in meaningful ways from other institutions. Hence, while making themselves aware of exemplary programs and practices, those charged with curricular reform should meet the task head-on, avoiding any "quick fixes" or ready-made solutions.

Pothole 3: Expect a holistic change.

Some committee members approach a curricular change assignment expecting to fashion a comprehensive program that will introduce revolutionary change all at once. To be sure, some institutions have created signature general education programs through curricular initiatives (consider the examples of Portland State University and Wagner College mentioned above). And some institutions, such as the experimental colleges formed during the 1960s or, more recently, California State University, Monterey Bay, have capitalized on once-in-a-lifetime opportunities for innovation. Other institutions have addressed crises through dramatic change. For instance, when Wilson College nearly closed in the early 1980s but instead evolved so as to serve a broader student clientele. But radical departures from established traditions are rare in the history of American higher education, and most changes are evolutionary, introduced incrementally and phased in over time (Hefferlin 1969). Furthermore, taking a holistic approach is a high-risk strategy. A comprehensive proposal takes a long time to fashion, yet a faculty can turn it down in a single meeting, thereby aborting the entire effort. In sum, a proposal designed to effect change through evolutionary action often offers a greater chance for acceptance—at least in part. Several committees that have seen their proposals rejected can attest to the practical wisdom of the maxim, "think comprehensively but act incrementally."

Pothole 4: Tinker with distribution requirements.

Amid the current debate about general education, one approach seeks to reinstate or revise conventional distribution requirements, which largely consist of mandates for introductory courses in traditional liberal arts disciplines taught by standard lecture or seminar methods. This approach may indeed improve the general education of students at some institutions, but it has three major limitations. First, although most institutions have had extensive experience with the distribution model, overreliance on distribution requirements has spawned many of the very problems that current reform efforts seek to overcome (Levine 1978). These problems include fragmentation of the curriculum, erosion of an accepted educational rationale, lack of commitment on the part of the faculty, loss of interest by students, and absence of any central administration or supervision of the general education program. Second, most people think of breadth of knowledge as only one component of general education. Acquiring various capacities such as communications, quantitative reasoning, and analysis is also very important. Finally, learning to integrate ideas and to apply learning across the various disciplines to address social and community problems are also important general outcomes of a college education. None of these components is necessarily well served by distribution requirements. Although studying a broad array of academic disciplines is common in virtually all general education programs, distribution requirements by themselves are rarely sufficient. In a faculty workshop at Weber State University, following the participation of a Weber team in a recent AAC&U Institute on General Education, the chair of the faculty senate declared bluntly of its distribution requirements, "we do not have a *program* of general education, and it is not assessable." That statement got the attention of everyone and gave impetus to assessment and curricular review initiatives.

Pothole 5: Capitulate to entrenched interests.

Curricular reform worthy of the name must not perpetuate the very problems that prompted reform in the first place: fragmentation of the curriculum through the proliferation of ever more highly specialized courses, a lack of enthusiasm for the program by both faculty and students, and a vacuum of ownership. When students routinely discuss the general education program as a set of requirements that must be endured before meaningful study can begin, it should be clear that the opportunity of a generation has been missed. For these reasons, the AAC&U Institute on General Education has discouraged campus teams from merely rearranging distribution requirements in deference to those protecting the status quo. Instead, the institute encourages teams to build curricula that offer the kind of education students will need for their futures.

Erroneous Task Force Procedures

Colleges and universities are organized to provide oversight of the instructional program, and they tend to utilize existing structures and procedures as they address general education. Curricular review groups often work through existing committees, without any special support, expecting curricular revision to be a short-term project. Instead, the process requires careful organization. An effective leader must be appointed. Respected faculty leaders must be recruited. There must be a clear charge and definitive parameters, a reasonable timeframe, and adequate support. In turn, members of the leadership group must prepare themselves by reading the professional literature, studying trends and innovations, and building their credibility as leaders among their colleagues. Otherwise, potholes may emerge.

Pothole 6: Work according to "business as usual" through the curriculum committee.

That curricular review should be conducted by the standing curriculum committee may seem reasonable. However, forming a special task force might be a better route to take. While a standing committee has its regular, time-consuming business to accomplish, a task force can devote all its energy to the single purpose of reviewing or revising the curriculum. In addition, unlike a special task force, a standing committee regularly changes its membership, and more than one group has found that new members can sidetrack its work by reintroducing issues and arguments settled earlier. Furthermore, curriculum committees, which traditionally react to proposals from faculty members or departments, may operate with a veto-power mentality to ensure that the curriculum does not get out of hand. By contrast, efforts to improve general education require that a group proactively develops a proposal and actively gathers campus support for its ideas. And such a group can draw on those most knowledgeable, most interested, and most committed. Moreover, a dedicated committee can work with less distraction, take advantage of opportunities for concentrated work such as that provided by the AAC&U Institute on General Education, and pursue a timeline more likely to bring results.

Pothole 7: Work without any special support.

Too many task forces try to effect massive curricular change without adequate support. This situation frequently occurs when the task is given to a standing committee, because such committees seldom receive any release time for their leaders or members, special budgets, or other assistance. We have learned that reduced teaching assignments can be essential, at least for a committee chair, if there is to be sufficient time and energy to provide leadership for curricular revision. A one- or two-course reduction in teaching assignments for the chairperson, summer stipends for members, and relief from other institutional service expectations are examples of support than can make a difference. Some institutions pay students for their committee contributions during the academic year or summer, and others structure the task force's work so that students can earn academic credit for assisting with it. Further, task forces need modest funds to purchase materials, hold retreats, invite consultants, reproduce papers for campus distribution, and, perhaps, send a team to the AAC&U Institute on General Education and similar meetings. Unless adequate support is given, a task force or committee cannot be expected to provide creative and effective leadership for curricular change. Allocating budget resources to this initiative is a major way in which academic administrators can demonstrate institutional support for educational improvement. Hence one of the first questions that a savvy task force should ask is, what support will our group require in order to be successful?

Pothole 8: Plan for a short-term project.

Many task group members engaged with general education reform may assume at first that their work will span only a few months. They then become frustrated and disappointed when the work takes much longer. There are examples of significant change in general education taking several years and a couple of special cases where it has been accomplished in just a few months. But our experience is that more commonly it takes two to three years for a faculty to reach agreement on student learning goals and to design a new curriculum that intentionally cultivates those qualities. Implementing a new program may take at least four more years. The process is faster if faculty members are knowledgeable about educational trends, issues, and innovations and if they have experience working with colleagues across the campus on these matters. Otherwise it may take even longer as they learn about each other and about each other's ideas and practices. Scheduling too little time for the process can convey a lack of appreciation both for the weight of the effort and for the limits inherent in an academic year calendar. (Because of start-up activities, exam preparations, and holidays, the typical academic year allows only about five months for productive faculty work on the curriculum.) General education committees would do well to keep in mind the dieter's dictum: fat that took years to put on cannot be removed in a few days. The difficulties surrounding general education are often so severe and deep-seated that they cannot be resolved overnight, and more time than is anticipated is often needed to rectify them.

Pothole 9: Use existing forums to discuss general education.

Faculties have many meetings to conduct their business, but few are well suited for the discussion of general education issues or the exploration of creative ideas for improvements. For instance, department meetings typically are focused on limited agendas rather than on institution-wide perspectives. Meetings of the faculty as a whole or of faculty senates tend to deal with business matters and rarely provide a good context to hold a collective intellectual inquiry about how to best prepare students for their futures. Meetings that are primarily political are not the best to elicit constructive thinking about the curriculum. Curriculum task forces have found that, in order to pursue serious and creative ideas, they often need to create new forums such as fall faculty development meetings, seminars, retreats, open hearings, and book discussions.

Pothole 10: Have the committee work in isolation to develop a proposal.

The rationale for issue-specific task forces is that they can probe a subject in depth and issue a report, which enables the larger group to make an informed decision without investing all of its time. This rationale has led some committees to work entirely in private. Its members survey the state of the art around the country, examine alternative forms of general education, discuss pros and cons of different models, and then release their recommendations to the faculty at large. The faculty may perceive such reports as coming out of the blue. Facing accusations of holding secret discussions, the faculty members on the committee may then feel that their assigned prerogative to be actively involved in curricular policy making has been ignored. An example of what can happen when a committee acts too abruptly appears in a 1996 report from California State University, Northridge, where a three-year general education reform effort ground to a halt, at least temporarily, because of complaints that faculty members "either had not seen a draft reform proposal or thought the draft was a done deal." The committee acted promptly in an effort to address the concerns, but not in time to keep the reform process on course. One faculty member commented that "if we try to push it before people are satisfied . . . there's going to be so much resistance [that] when it goes to the Senate it's going to go down in flames" (Chandler 1996).

By contrast, there is the example of the strategic, sequential approach at St. Cloud State University, where the general education committee first developed and proposed for approval a general education mission statement. With that approval in hand, the committee then "worked with over 100 SCSU faculty volunteers to draft a set of student learning outcomes." Following the work of the volunteers, the committee reported significant progress and invited departmental representatives to "January Workshop Days" and to "Reading Circles" focused on "general education goal areas." At that point, the intent of the university "to invigorate, improve, and strengthen our General Education Curriculum" appeared well on its way to fulfillment. By January 2007, the university had approved a general education assessment plan, initiated a search for an assessment director, and completed its statement of goals and student learning outcomes. (For a more detailed overview, see www.stcloudstate.edu/generaleducation/docpolicies.) Not everyone needs to travel every mile, but effective general education reform committees reach out, include, and inform as many as possible in the work they are doing. One principle behind the AAC&U Institute on General Education is that there can be great value in the concerted work of small committees so long as they keep in mind the vital importance of building constituency support.

Pothole 11: Issue a single final report.

When writing scholarly papers, academics typically wait until their ideas are fully developed and well expressed before submitting papers for publication or other critical scrutiny by their colleagues. Applying this commonsense approach to the preparation of a curricular proposal can be catastrophic. More than one institution has had a committee working laboriously for years to develop an elegant and comprehensive proposal. The documents, although lengthy, have been impressive in their philosophy of education, analysis of the institution, and number of recommendations. Unfortunately, they often contain something for everyone to dislike and are thus greeted by a chorus of opposition. Other groups find they are more successful when they issue a progressive series of reports followed by conversations to secure agreement on, for example, learning goals for students, common educational principles, and curricular themes. Only later does a comprehensive curricular proposal emerge.

For instance, at Southern Illinois University Edwardsville, the movement toward reform began with the committee's inviting proposals from potentially hundreds of colleagues. With the active support of the faculty senate, the committee then led a campus-wide effort to select three "finalist" proposals to be considered in depth during a daylong meeting of all faculty members. From the discussion and an ensuing referendum emerged a consensus intended to serve as the basis for eventual implementation. The University of Nebraska–Lincoln's general education reform Web site (www.unl.edu/svcaa/gened) is a good example of how the Web can be used to ensure sustained communication. Following a list of proposals under consideration—which refer to specific student learning outcomes and "structural criteria"—are "frequently asked questions," overviews of current and former reform efforts, a list of those consulted, a glossary, and a list of resources. The site also makes clear what work remains to be done. Similar elements appear also in the procedure followed by Butler University as its faculty developed a distinctive general education program. Such a procedure has the advantage of involving the faculty at each step along the way as the task force leads the faculty progressively through the task of developing a full proposal.

Pothole 12: Assume that reform can't be implemented because of any of a number of reasons.

When institutions of higher learning encounter difficulties, faculty members' morale may drop as they become pessimistic about their ability to make any significant change in the educational program. For example, Portland State, mentioned above as an exemplar of innovative curricular reform, was prior to the 1990s an unremarkable regional state university in a region suffering from a serious economic downturn. There was no prospect of significant additional state funds. But in 1992, the president and provost, with the support of key faculty leaders, decided that they would be better off if they were to take the initiative to determine their own future. The administration supported the faculty as it crafted a very different general education program guided by educational research. The resulting program, implemented in 1994, features interdisciplinary learning communities, creates a greater presence in the Portland community, and supports assessment of learning. This program has resulted in greater enrollment, higher graduation rates, documented improvements in learning, and considerable national recognition in the form of awards and grants. In short, Portland State made lemonade out of the lemons it had been given (White 1994). Similar stories can be told about Hamline University and, as noted above, about Wagner College and Elon University. If significant reform can happen in places facing serious problems, it surely can happen in many other less challenged institutions. Members of productive groups tend to take a practical stance and focus on "what we can do here using our own resources" rather than wringing their hands and assuming failure.

Pothole 13: Ignore the role of students.

Faculty members typically regard the development of the curriculum as their prerogative and sometimes neglect the important contributions students can make to the process. Students are typically quite interested in any effort to change the curriculum, especially as such changes may affect graduation requirements. We typically recommend that students be appointed to the leadership group, but at the very least the task force needs to enlist students to offer their views of their curricular experiences, help study the operation of the current curriculum, research innovations at other institutions, and help with communications with the student body. More than one institution has discovered that the student voice can be a potent force, for good or ill, in affecting the outcome of a curricular initiative.

The Big Question: What Is General Education?

Discussions of general education can often elicit the best—and sometimes the worst—in members of the academy. At best, such discussions draw on deeply held convictions about desirable learning outcomes, capacities for learning, effective pedagogies, and approaches to assessment. At worst, they can degenerate into endless quibbling over definitions. Effective committees refer often to emerging areas of consensus as they move from conceptual to more practical stages of discussion. As noted above, one succinct expression of consensus that has proved useful in a variety of situations is the one-page summary published by AAC&U (see appendix B). Titled "Essential Learning Outcomes," the outline expresses the now widely shared conviction that students should prepare for twenty-first-century challenges by gaining knowledge of human cultures and the physical and natural world, intellectual and practical skills, personal and social responsibility, and integrative learning that includes the opportunity to address "complex problems." Brief bulleted lists, in turn, further define each category. As mentioned above, some institutions have expedited the process of reform by regarding this broad vision of the academy as a point of departure. However, others continue to encounter the familiar potholes that follow.

Pothole 14: Seek the one true meaning of general education.

Each committee member tends to vest his or her own definition with unmerited authority. Naturally, different concepts, strongly held, can lead to disagreements and even conflicts. After hearing members articulate their views over and over again, some members lament that the group cannot even agree on the meaning of general education, let alone on ways to strengthen it. Eventually the committee may realize that the term is fraught with ambiguity, that it admits several definitions, and that each person may have a legitimate claim to his or her own view. Once accepting this reality, the committee is in a position to adopt a *provisional* definition, attempt to explore and elaborate its meaning as work progresses, and seek to understand the assumptions and values that underlie the various concepts of general education. The committee will likely have a richer sense of the meaning of the term at the conclusion of their efforts than at the outset.

Pothole 15: Assume general education involves only breadth of knowledge.

This common presupposition tends to be associated with the notion that students should be introduced to an array of academic disciplines. Few would dispute the contention that breadth of knowledge is part of general education. However, in addition to breadth of knowledge, learning skills and integration of knowledge are now widely regarded as important components of general education. As soon as a committee learns to substitute *a* definition for *the* definition of general education, it is free to consider various ways to enhance all elements of the curriculum. Indeed, as our earlier concern with reforms limited to revision of distribution requirements may have suggested, many argue that a core curriculum addressing common needs, concerns, and themes through interdisciplinary courses is likely to prove more productive than such requirements (Boyer and Kaplan 1977).

Pothole 16: View general education as only cognitive in character.

The starting place for many faculty members is asking the reasonable question, what knowledge should a generally educated person have? The ensuing consideration of which disciplines are the most basic or important then leads naturally and directly to legendary battles over "turf." Some committees have found that they can avoid these difficulties by seeking to identify the qualities, not only the knowledge, that mark the generally educated person. At the University of Oregon, for instance, the goals of general education go beyond important cognitive knowledge to include "personal development and an expanded view of self." And at Southern Methodist University (SMU), such development represents the *highest* priority. SMU seeks "to educate its students as worthy human beings and as citizens, first, and as teachers, lawyers, ministers, research scientists, businessmen, engineers, and so on, second." Thus, many affective qualities, attitudes, values, and skills can be goals of general education; purely cognitive knowledge, however important, accounts for only some of the attributes of an educated person.

Pothole 17: Regard general education as only curricular.

Often, the question of what knowledge a student should possess leads to questions that are solely curricular: how many courses should there be in each subject area, and what should each accomplish? But general education outcomes may arise from a variety of noncurricular sources as well. Hence, reform committees are wise to acknowledge that enthusiasm for learning, respect for personal relationships, and awareness of one's examined values may be learned even more effectively through extracurricular experience within the academic community, residential life, and the broader region. At Eastern Michigan University (EMU), the general education program implemented in 2006 is explicitly "about more than just classes." According to EMU, "students involved in activities outside of the classroom have higher retention rates and more positive educational experiences. Learning beyond the classroom encourages students to obtain hands-on experience and to learn about professionalism; it also provides a way to apply classroom knowledge." Broadening the conversation about general education has the additional advantage of drawing others to it, especially those student affairs professionals who might otherwise remain on the sidelines.

Pothole 18: Assume liberal arts and sciences faculties to be the sole defenders of general education.

A pernicious myth within general education reform is that liberal arts faculties are beleaguered defenders of culture and general education against infidels in the professional and practical arts. To the contrary, the broad consensus outlined in AAC&U's *Taking Responsibility for the Quality of the Baccalaureate Degree* (2004) emphasizes that responsibility for general education is broadly shared by all faculty, both those in the arts and sciences and those in the professions. This report of the Project on Accreditation and Assessment, which was initiated by AAC&U in 2000, reflects the involvement of regional accrediting agencies, four specialized accreditors, several educational associations committed to liberal learning, and a number of faculty members and academic administrators. In essence, the report calls for a coherent baccalaureate curriculum with "an engaging beginning that captures the interest of students and provides insight into the ways scholars in [each] field of study think and create knowledge." Then a "purposeful" middle should lead to "cumulative and deeper learning." Finally, a culminating experience should offer an opportunity for integration and for substantive creation (8). In this light, general education becomes not a discrete academic bailiwick, but rather an integral part of a larger whole that is "purposeful," "coherent," "engaging," and "rigorous" (9). Extending throughout the baccalaureate, effective general education should enjoy strong leadership, sufficient resources, and, perhaps most importantly, the broad support of all faculty. "The faculty as a whole must agree on the purpose, structure, and content of general education, aid its implementation, and participate in its assessment" (9). Although, as the report concedes, "a balkanized approach to general education still prevails among most faculty members, students, and advisors," a priority of any general education reform committee must be to approach general education as a vital element within an "integrated, holistic approach to the curriculum," one engaging both liberal arts and professional program faculty (11).

Pothole 19: Identify humanists as the only true believers in general education.

This variation of Pothole 18 goes so far as to identify scientists and other professionals as opponents of curricular breadth. But as long ago as 1978, a study at the State University of New York at Buffalo (SUNYAB) concluded that students in the sciences were more likely to choose electives in the humanities than students majoring in the humanities were to choose electives in the sciences: "In the fall of 1977, English majors at SUNYAB took only 3.5 percent of their courses in natural sciences, mathematics, health sciences, or engineering. This matches, almost exactly, the proportion of engineering students taking courses in arts and letters and is significantly less than the comparable figures for students in health science and management majors." If anything, that trend has since become even more pronounced. The appropriate response to this canard is the same as that to intransigent defenders of an insular liberal arts faith: rather than polarizing the faculty by pointing at "good guys" and "bad guys," many committees have found it productive to assume that general education is a priority for all fields of study and for all types of students. This reasonable position allows them to consider how faculty from all fields can improve course offerings. And they will find ready allies in the accreditors of professional programs. For instance, ABET—the recognized accreditor for college and university programs in applied science, computing, engineering, and technology—requires that programs provide students with "an understanding of professional and ethical responsibility, an ability to communicate effectively, the broad education necessary to understand the impact of engineering solutions in a global, economic, environmental, and societal context, a recognition of the need for, and an ability to engage in life-long learning, and a knowledge of contemporary issues" (2007). Similarly, the Association to Advance Collegiate Schools of Business specifies that undergraduate degree programs should provide business students with "communication abilities, ethical understanding and reasoning abilities, analytic skills, [the ability to use] information technology, multicultural and diversity understanding, and reflective thinking skills—all staples of general education as well as the business professions" (AACSB International 2007).

Pothole 20: Integration is a responsibility appropriately left to students themselves.

Nearly everyone agrees that students should not merely master discrete bits of knowledge but integrate them as well. While that agreement may receive eloquent expression in printed descriptions of general education curricula, some faculty members appear content to leave this responsibility to students. Hence Jonathan Smith, former dean of the college at the University of Chicago, once declared an "iron law": "students shall not be expected to integrate anything the faculty can't or won't" (pers. comm.). His edict makes sense, because integration is not likely to occur unless it is made a priority within curricular planning and embedded in the structure of the academic program. For this to occur, faculty members from different academic disciplines must engage in dialogue over substantive issues and build an academic community to sustain their general education program. In their article "Integrative Learning for Liberal Education," Huber, Hutchings, and Gale (2005, 4–5), acknowledging the long lineage of the "goal" of integrated learning, observe that "what's new today is that institutions are seeking to help students see the larger patterns in their college experience, and to pursue their learning in more intentionally connected ways. To put it a bit differently, the capacity for integrative learning—for connection making—has come to be recognized as an important learning outcome in its own right, not simply a hoped-for consequence of the mix of experiences that constitute undergraduate education." Committees intent on genuine curricular reform should aspire to no less. In short, if the committee regards the integration of learning as a curricular objective, it must make it clear how students will achieve this objective. Otherwise, a looming pothole will separate desirable ends from wholly inadequate means.

Mistakes to Avoid in Program Planning

Both of the authors have received calls from leaders of curricular initiatives with urgent requests for advice: "How can we get 'them' to approve 'our' proposal?" Of course, by then it is too late, because the way to get "them" to approve a proposal is to engage them in devising it. The task force needs to involve the faculty with repeated communications about various topics, issue frequent progress reports, solicit the views of colleagues, and operate an open, inclusive process. Otherwise, potholes may lie ahead.

Pothole 21: Seek to continue the process of change by addition.

In the days of expanding institutions and expansive budgets, much academic change was accomplished by adding new programs, securing larger budgets, recruiting more students, and hiring more instructors. Today, this avenue is closed off at most institutions. Instead, new programs are now being introduced through shifts in priorities, reallocation of resources, reassignment of faculty members, and expansion of the professional competencies of existing personnel. Although a much more complicated route to reform than change by addition, it is the only road available to most schools. Hence a committee dedicated to strengthening general education must often face these facts. While committee members may believe that an expanded general education program would serve students better, unless they can establish at the start that expansion would be feasible, the committee should avoid the pothole of frustrated ambitions and give its attention to more realistic options.

Pothole 22: Limit the debate to the campus.

Many committees begin their deliberations by having members share their best ideas for improving general education. This approach can pool a great deal of ignorance and half-truths, and it frequently results in premature polarization of the group. By contrast, other task forces have embarked on a scholarly exploration of the topic and have consciously cultivated a spirit of inquiry so that each person learns to expand, refine, and alter his or her initial ideas. These task forces read the literature, secure a consultant or two, attend a conference or workshop, or visit other institutions. One good example of the scholarly approach may be seen in the colorful and eclectic Web site of the general education reform effort at the University of California at Santa Barbara (www.history.ucsb.edu/projects/ge). The site provides references to newspaper editorials and to the general education requirements of other California institutions as well as links to a broad range of exemplary general education programs throughout the nation. Similarly, a committee at the University of Tennessee committee created a series of faculty study groups and provided participants with a few key volumes to read and discuss. In both cases, the development of specific proposals was not pursued until the faculty had developed a level of sophistication on the topic of general education.

Pothole 23: Resist the combining of change strategies and exclude those who have been innovating in related areas.

Too often, curricular task forces reflect the appointment of the "usual suspects." While it is important that general education reform involve acknowledged campus leaders, it is no less important that committees include individuals from critical but less traditional areas. Those engaged in freshman seminars, in across-the-curriculum initiatives in writing or mathematics, in diversity initiatives, and in international studies, to mention just a few, can offer valuable guidance in the development of a genuinely comprehensive proposal. These individuals have actual experience, not just ideas and aspirations, of what works—and what does not—that can contribute to the development of a realistic as well as ambitious proposal. Betty Schmitz (1992) argues for incorporating into the change process all who have been working in related areas, including writing, women's studies, and learning communities. Leaders of these initiatives have experiences and expertise that can be utilized in changing the curriculum.

Pothole 24: Rely on "autobiographical" proposals.

Writing for the American Association of Community Colleges, William J. Flynn (2005, 9) endorses the influential observation of Lee Knefelkamp that the curriculum often embodies the "collective autobiography of the faculty." The faculty, Flynn continues, "have a heavy intellectual and emotional investment in the current curriculum. . . . Because their primary allegiance is to their department or discipline, there is little or no sense of the collective whole, no meaningful comprehension of the overall process of a student's education. Taken collectively, the curriculum is enormous and compartmentalized, tied to its contributing departments. To the student, the curriculum is incoherent and unwieldy, and stands as an impediment to intellectual achievement or academic progress." This describes well a problem most curricular reformers are determined to ameliorate. Yet innovators may find that faculty members, because they tend not to be connected with the national dialogue about curricular matters, offer ideas that are largely autobiographical. Although good ideas may arise from personal experience, the danger is that faculty members will prescribe for today's students what was done for (or to) them in their own general education. Groups that encourage members to transcend personal experience have a better chance of designing programs that are responsive to the interests of today's students and to contemporary realities.

Pothole 25: Ignore the abundance of research that shows what educational conditions engage students and enhance their learning.

Savvy committees understand that no curriculum can be more effective than the means through which it is offered. In other words, those interested in reform must give as much attention to teaching and learning as to curricular design. Fortunately, there has emerged a substantial literature that embodies important knowledge about how students learn and how learning can be improved. That literature has influenced general education reform at James Madison University (JMU), for example. Having agreed that the curriculum alone would not ensure effective general education, the JMU faculty considered how pedagogy might reflect "a philosophy that promotes the cultivation of habits of the mind and heart that are essential to the functioning of informed citizens in a democracy and world community." Hence the faculty have pursued a commitment to a paradigm shift, from "teaching students" to "encouraging students to become active in their own education and deliberate in making good choices for themselves and in connections with others."

Pothole 26: Assume that the committee knows the experiences and views of relevant constituencies.

Because members of a committee are from the campus, they may presume to be—and are often presumed to be—aware of faculty and student perspectives throughout the campus. Because this is not always the case, some committees have found it instructive to conduct studies to test their preconceived ideas. And some have reached surprising conclusions! The State University of New York at Buffalo study mentioned above is one such example. Another is the Rochester Institute of Technology, which, as an aid to planning, surveyed its students, faculty members, and alumni as well as members of the local community.

Pothole 27: Stick with a "rational" plan despite changing circumstances.

Virtually all rational planning models call for planners to specify goals, assess needs, determine alternatives, design and implement a program, and evaluate outcomes. Hence teams are well advised to choose at the outset a rational, systematic approach to reform. Yet for a variety of circumstances, effective programs have been fashioned in many different ways. And change does not always have to be systemic in order to be influential. For example, during the 1980s Columbia University created a series of "teaching companies"—upper-division interdisciplinary study groups—by having faculty members identify common interests that transcend their disciplines and by devising new courses on such topics. The university built part of the program around the intellectual interests of faculty, rather than following the usual practice of recruiting faculty to staff courses conceived in the abstract.

Pothole 28: Search for the "one best" program.

There is a current cliché: "don't let the perfect become the enemy of the good." That can be wise advice for a curricular reform committee. Sometimes there arises a commitment to building a curriculum that will stand as an enduring monument to its creators. A more humble assumption, that a curriculum should represent a university's best effort at a given moment, can prompt reform that is timely. A faculty member from Baker College at the 2008 Institute on General Education commented that there is less pressure to build a curriculum if the task is seen as one of building for a period of time, rather than "for all time." It is enough to create a sound program that continues to grow and evolve.

Pothole 29: Keep the committee out of politics.

This can appear a laudable objective. But the general education reform committee at Southern Illinois University Edwardsville, which we mention more than once, sought instead to engage the political process from the start. In its first announcement, the chair of the reform promised that the committee would not "cook up a single General Education plan and seek to impose it on the faculty. Rather it will oversee the development (and solicitation) of a number of plans and will help guide a broad conversation that will lead to the adoption of one of (or some hybrid of) the plans." By recognizing that any university is, among other things, a political entity, the committee chose a strategy that would uncover the preferences of various groups so that their views might be incorporated into the process. Hence the committee was able to build coalitions and to demonstrate how the interests of various departments and other campus groups might be served by the various proposals that resulted.

Pothole 30: Couch proposals in the jargon of innovation.

As curricular reform committee members become engaged with the literature of innovation, they naturally become inclined to use the language of such literature in their reports and written materials. But this rhetoric may in fact create resistance to change among those unfamiliar with it. Hence some groups have chosen to heed the venerable lesson cited by A. Lawrence Lowell in his 1938 book, *What a University President Has Learned*: "If he desires to innovate he will be greatly helped by having the reputation of being conservative, because the radicals who want a change are little offended by the fact of change, while the conservatives will be likely to follow him because they look on him as sharing their temperament and point of view." Proposals that seem to advocate a return to fundamental purposes and procedures rather than a radical departure from present practices may draw support from both liberal and conservative campus groups.

Securing Approval of Proposals

Many task forces begin their work without knowing who precisely must approve any change they may propose. Do part-time faculty vote, or only full time? Must the faculty as a whole weigh in, or only the faculty senate? Some leaders bring a proposal to the faculty, and if there is no vocal opposition, they assume they have (and will continue to enjoy) approval. But many have discovered that silence may not signify consent. Whatever body must approve, its leaders should be informed regularly of the progress of the task force and their advice solicited throughout the process. Otherwise, the following familiar potholes may jar the unwary.

Pothole 31: Have the committee play a passive role in the debate and approval process.

Some committees adopt the scholarly model of publishing their best thinking and waiting for the reviews and reactions from their professional colleagues. The faculty must have a full and fair debate on the issues, of course, but several task forces have learned that they must take an active part in the debate and guide the approval process if their proposals are to have any chance of passing. The role of the committee thus shifts from that of a studying and recommending body to that of an advocate for the proposals. After all, if the committee members will not speak for their own recommendations, who will? The faculty has only a few months to process all the issues, problems, recommendations, and rationales that the committee may have grappled with for years. Committee members can greatly aid the approval process by initiating conversations with key people such as committee chairpersons, department chairpersons, faculty leaders, and deans—and by making themselves visible in meetings convened to consider the proposals.

Pothole 32: Present the proposal in an open hearing.

In the throes of promising general education reform, a task force may find itself increasingly tempted to schedule an open hearing on campus for interested faculty members in order to present the task force's best thinking for colleagues to critique. But the good ideas entertained within the task force, grown out of constructive and enjoyable discussions, might not fare well in an open hearing. When faculty colleagues are asked for a critique, they often criticize a proposal—sometimes sharply—even if they do not fully understand it. Hence it may be wiser to share the spirit of the retreat by scheduling several small-group meetings before attempting an open hearing. Although time consuming, this technique could succeed in engaging more people in thinking about how to enhance the quality of general education and lay the groundwork for subsequent efforts.

Pothole 33: **Seek approval of a comprehensive proposal.**

A word to wise committees: when appropriate, disaggregate. Although a comprehensive proposal can generate a coalition of opposition, some of its recommendations may be accepted if they are debated and acted upon separately. Some schools have divided a comprehensive proposal into separate portions that are brought before the faculty. An alternate approach that we have mentioned is to bring not one, but several comprehensive proposals before the faculty. That is, the committee may choose to be identified not as the advocate for a single proposal, but rather as the facilitator for a decision among alternatives that is the faculty's to make.

Pothole 34: **Avoid and isolate opponents.**

Because avoiding persons who disagree with one is human nature, committee members may be tempted to isolate and ignore their critics. While this may be a good short-term strategy, ignoring critics does not make them go away; indeed, they may become more persistent and vocal. Some committees have deputized members or small delegations to meet quietly with these critics, hear their concerns, and either incorporate features that respond to their concerns or explain why that cannot be done. This procedure may improve the proposal as well as silence some of the opposition. Of course, some loud, persistent, and disruptive individuals may continue to obstruct the work of the task force. After repeated efforts to hear their concerns, the task force may find it necessary to ignore and isolate them. Some of these individuals may eventually come around and be supportive, especially if they see their colleagues on the side of a new curriculum.

Pothole 35: **Assume that any opposition is irrational.**

Some committee members may have difficulty acknowledging that there may be good reasons for opposing new policies to strengthen general education. Even potential supporters may have legitimate concerns. Therefore, some groups go out of their way to reassure faculty members that the group's proposals to strengthen undergraduate education are not, for example, antithetical to specialization, a threat to graduate education, contrary to the interests of departments, or a way to rid the institution of some faculty members. Some committee reports make it clear that not all faculty members would be involved in teaching new courses, and other reports insist that resources be available to assist faculty members in adjusting to new courses and the new program. At times, creative responses to vocal opposition can make all the difference in gaining approval of a proposal.

Pothole 36: Fail to consider legitimate fears.

Any general education reform may promise changes that appear threatening to programs, departments, or individuals. Unless the committee can provide reassurance, it can probably count on opposition. While a committee may not be able to provide blanket protection for all, some have found it useful to secure from the administration a promise that, for a fixed period of time, no positions will be lost as a result of proposed curricular changes. In addition, the availability of funds to help faculty members develop new knowledge and skills to participate in the program can go a long way to allay fears and concerns.

Pothole 37: Assume that the faculty members understand the proposals.

It is essential to educate faculty members about a proposed program by distributing a written report and holding discussions. Yet, rare is the vote that takes place without at least some people having misunderstood portions of the proposal. Some opposition may thus arise from simple misinformation about the current situation, the proposed improvements, the implications for other parts of the institution, and the like. In an effort to ensure that nobody votes on the basis of misinformation, a committee may assign individuals to talk with known opponents. It is always in the committee's interest to make sure that its opponents are genuinely in disagreement, rather than merely misinformed. Alternatively, a proposal may be discussed in one or more meetings where no vote is taken as a means of helping to educate the community about the details before an actual vote is recorded.

Pothole 38: Assume that logic will prevail.

If a plan for curricular reform is all that brilliant minds can make it, should it not be able to stand on its own and persuade the academic community through the force of its ideas? The answer is yes—and no. As Lee G. Bolman and Terrence E. Deal (1991) have observed in a seminal study, organizations do not always function as well-oiled machines operating in orderly ways to produce predictable outcomes. Most organizations are, in some sense, also families. They present "family pride," domestic tensions, and no lack of internal rivalries. Organizations can be "jungles" also, environments where real and imagined issues become bones of contention and where only the most fully supported ideas survive. And organizations are "theaters" where symbols matter and the command of center stage can be crucial. What is happening in objective terms may matter less to an audience than "what it all means." Hence committees, keeping in mind the complexity of the organization they seek to persuade, must be willing to take into account not only any rational concerns that may be voiced, but also any family tensions, anxieties, rivalries, and personal histories that may influence the consideration.

Pothole 39: Use regular voting procedures.

Some task forces never question in advance a business-as-usual approach for voting on a major curricular proposal. Indeed, on the premise that a revised curriculum should enjoy broad faculty support, some institutions may demand a "supermajority" for curricular proposals. The stakes can rise even higher if abstentions relative to a fixed majority are to be tallied as "no" votes. Precisely because curricular reform should stand on its merits, without attracting whatever political baggage may be present in the environment, there can be some advantage to seeking approval through a dedicated process discrete from traditional governance procedures. A referendum by mail is one such method. Of course, because alternative approval methods would have to win the support of faculty governance, a reform task force cannot begin too early to ensure the backing of colleagues.

Pothole 40: Agree to a definitive vote after a "reasonable time for discussion."

This method seems to be sensible; however, after a task force has spent years working on a proposal and holding extended discussions with the faculty, scheduling a definitive vote could be suicidal if the outcome were in doubt. In such instances, further discussion and negotiation may keep the proposal alive until a few more advocates can be gained. The Machiavellian answer to the question of when to put the proposal to a vote is, "when the votes are assured."

Pothole 41: Assume a negative vote is final.

The road to curricular reform is strewn with abandoned vehicles that have fallen into the deepest of potholes, that of interpreting a negative vote as the end of the road. Prudent committees prepare for every eventuality, including that of rejection. In the aftermath of a negative vote, a committee should expand rather than close the lines of communication. As one strategy, it might ask opponents of its proposal to state in writing specific problems and to propose specific ways the proposal might be modified to overcome their objections. Or the committee might choose to expand its ranks, drawing from areas where there was strong support for the committee's recommendations as well as from areas where there was opposition. Third, a committee could signal its commitment to persevere by scheduling another vote to follow its revision efforts. As one expression of this strategy, a curricular reform committee might declare in advance of a faculty referendum that a negative vote would not put the committee out of business, but rather return it to the drawing board.

Pothole 42: Ignore the possibility that the proposal might be used as a surrogate for some other issue.

A savvy committee will keep its ear to the ground, lest consideration of its proposal be hijacked as an avenue to express views on some other issue. Facing a highly charged political atmosphere created by an unpopular administrator or a sharp reduction in travel funds, for instance, a committee may find it prudent to defer consideration until the dust has settled. Even in the Congress, experienced legislators avoid scheduling debates when the deliberative environment seems inopportune.

Program Implementation

Since the task of developing a proposal for change and securing approval is so laborious, it is understandable that curriculum task force members are eager to turn its implementation over to others. But the reality is that by the time the proposal is approved, the members are the most knowledgeable and committed faculty, and they often are asked to play leadership roles in implementing the whole program or significant portions of it. And in addition to a curriculum, there needs to be a plan for staffing, faculty and course development, administrative leadership, and assessment.

Pothole 43: The task force should issue a report for others to implement.

The process of planning a program is so demanding and time consuming that a committee may be eager to turn the responsibility for implementation over to somebody else. However, if the committee members and their institution are to realize the gains to which they aspire, they may have to invest in the implementation and maintenance of the program. In fact, more than one chair of a curricular review committee has accepted an invitation to serve as the director of the new program after it has been approved by the faculty. This may make sense, because that person is typically perceived as the most knowledgeable and effective spokesperson for general education and is regarded as the one most likely to oversee its effective implementation. Furthermore, committee members frequently end up teaching courses in the new program and helping to recruit colleagues to teach with them. Indeed, they are likely to find that the program operates best when they take an active part in its implementation.

Pothole 44: Assume there is no need for a staffing plan.

Who will teach in the new program? The more far-reaching the changes to be implemented, the more challenging it may be to ensure that all sections are staffed and appropriately taught. Ideally, the senior faculty will provide leadership by teaching core courses. The committee can tackle this concern directly, if that seems prudent, by making certain that the issue is among those discussed within the academic community and by engaging scheduling officers (chairs, deans, registrar, etc.) in planning for appropriate staffing and delivery. Even if it wins universal acclaim at the outset, the new curriculum will encounter formidable implementation potholes if there are too few full-time faculty members to offer courses—or if those willing to participate do not include a good number of senior faculty. The delegation of responsibility for teaching courses largely to adjunct faculty or teaching assistants is a bad omen.

Pothole 45: Ignore the priority any new program places on faculty development.

Effective faculty development enables those who are to teach the revised curriculum to prepare to do so (Meacham 2001). But it is important that opportunities for professional growth avoid the Scylla and Charybdis of patronization and the appearance of coercion. Strong development programs persuade successful scholars that they offer something worth knowing. For example, the National Academy for Academic Leadership has listed important questions worth posing to faculty members who seek to become better teachers (Gardiner 2000). If a reformed general education program is to succeed, the faculty teaching within it will have to recognize the necessary alignment between the "educational processes" they use and the "competency outcomes" they will seek. And in most instances, this recognition should prompt them to acquire the additional professional knowledge and skill competencies required for the appropriate educational processes. Once prompted to seek such development, a faculty member must encounter credible professionals who will respect her or his time, status within the academy, and professional accomplishments. For example, a faculty development day at Central Washington University focused on effective teaching within the general education program by going directly to the heart of the matter. Choosing as its point of departure Jerry Gaff's brief "reality check" essay, "Keeping General Education Vital: A Struggle Against Original Sin?" the organizers faced squarely the dangerous disciplinary undertow that threatens general education: "Academic pride,. . . the tendency of faculty to focus on their own discipline, research interests, and individual autonomy rather than on the most fundamental knowledge and skills their students need from a curriculum" (2003, 31). In that context, teams of faculty members framed statements of desired educational outcomes and proposed strategies that would support their accomplishment. One presentation on "Patterns and Connections in the Natural World" proposed interdisciplinary integration as a program priority and urged the abandonment of departmental designations and the creation of interdisciplinary learning communities.

Pothole 46: Ignore the reward structure.

Just because the faculty approves a new program does not necessarily mean that faculty members are willing to teach in it. Hence a further requisite is a closer alignment between the value the institution attaches to general education and the rewards it offers to those who teach within it. At the very least, effective teaching within the general education curriculum must not function as an impediment to acquiring tenure, promotion, or increases in compensation. But, ideally, those who distinguish themselves in such teaching will qualify for particular recognition. The profound influence of Ernest Boyer's and Eugene Rice's broader definitions of scholarship has reminded both institutions and faculty members alike that an inquisitive, intentional approach to teaching may itself be evaluated as a "scholarship" no less compelling for purposes of professional advancement than the more traditional scholarships of discovery, integration, and application (Boyer 1990; Rice 1991; Glassick, Huber, and Maeroff 1997; Edgerton, O'Meara, and Rice 2005).

Pothole 47: Assume that anybody can teach general education courses.

Courses that stress skills rather than content, range beyond disciplinary boundaries, or deal with value implications of knowledge pose challenges for any teacher, and such courses can be especially difficult for teachers who are cut from a traditional mold. In such instances, investment in professional development can become especially important. At Central Michigan University, an ambitious faculty development "curriculum" provides "discussion clusters" on such topics as "interdisciplinarity" and "integrated learning," presentations by faculty who have successfully developed courses qualifying for general education credit, and all-day "mini-institutes" the encourage deep knowledge of the general education program.

Pothole 48: Insist that the entire program be implemented at once.

Some committees expect that once the program is approved, it can be implemented in one fell swoop. But at some institutions, such as North Carolina Agricultural and Technical State University, an incremental, phased approach, beginning with the 2005–06 academic year, has worked well. Other schools, such as Bucknell University and Sonoma State University, have offered pilot programs involving a few faculty members and students prior to full implementation.

Pothole 49: Take it for granted that the program will work well the first time.

After investing so much time and energy in developing a new curriculum, committee members naturally have high expectations, but the expectations may be *too* high. A committee member does not have to accept Murphy's Law—"If something can go wrong, it will"—in order to realize that any new program will encounter some difficulties. Personnel problems, misunderstandings, personality conflicts, logistics, and other difficulties cannot all be avoided, even with the best advanced planning. Many institutions have discovered the wisdom of pilot-testing courses and components before they are offered as formal requirements. The first time courses, programs, or services are offered on a permanent basis, program implementers might preserve their mental health by conceiving of the offerings as a trial run with the goal of improving the operation on succeeding trials.

Pothole 50: Regard assessment as someone else's job.

While for many institutions assessment may provide the impetus for initiating curricular reform, its importance in the early stages of a newly implemented program can be even greater. As was clear as far back as 1980, there are political points to be gained when those responsible for a new program pursue an explicit commitment to its objective, actionable assessment. But because assessment within the past two decades has increasingly been driven by external mandates, the real challenge for an institution may be to develop an approach to assessment that is as faithful as possible to the values of the institution, that reflects the learning outcomes chosen by the institution for its general education program, and that produces visible results. It is important in this regard to distinguish the assessment that individual faculty members undertake to ensure their students are achieving the intended learning outcomes from those undertaken by the program or institution to measure, as it is described at Ferris State University, "the impact of the general education curriculum as a whole."

The approach at Ferris State is multifaceted, as effective assessment programs must be. Administration of "Academic Profiles" aspires to "a direct measure of student learning" through "a standardized comparison of entering and upper-level students." By generating scores both on students' academic skills and on their knowledge of the sciences, humanities, and social sciences, the approach measures their "progress toward meeting the learning outcomes in . . . Reading, Reasoning Ability, Quantitative Skills, Scientific Understanding, Cultural Enrichment, and Social Awareness." A "College Student Experience Questionnaire" provides an "indirect measure of student learning." The program also employs the National Survey of Student Engagement and recommends other assessment methods specific to particular outcomes. From this thorough approach, Ferris State achieves "a fuller picture of the knowledge and skills of both entering and exiting students" so that the university can "really understand what students need, what they learn, what they don't learn, and what we need to do to improve the general education learning opportunities." The Collegiate Learning Assessment developed by the Council for Aid to Education offers a further option for some institutions.

In Summary

Those considering or already engaged in the reform of general education will have by this point gained a renewed appreciation for the hazards that await the drivers of curricular change. They will have heard of some promising models, and they will have gained sensitivity to both the extent and the importance of their task. But before turning the key in the ignition, they should do one more walk-around, one more scan of the instrument panel, one more review of the "six basic ideas" set forth in 1980. (A brief digest of our positive recommendations appears in appendix A.) First, potholes should be expected because the task of reconstructing the general education program of a college or university is difficult and complicated. Second, no one piloting a curricular proposal down the road toward approval can expect to miss all the holes in the road; even the best driver is jarred occasionally. Third, hitting a pothole or two can slow the pace, but it will seldom knock the vehicle off course. Fourth, falling into too many potholes can make people take another road altogether (or, if care is not taken, abandon the entire journey). Fifth, alternative routes can be bumpy, too, so the best route may be the original one rather than the suggested alternative. Finally, avoiding potholes is an art; it involves some luck, but one's skill can—and should—discernibly improve.

Appendix A
Pothole Patches

Strategies for Avoiding or Overcoming Impediments to Curricular Reform

1. Help your colleagues understand the significance of general education, and acquaint them with an emerging consensus about critical learning goals.

2. Make it clear that general education must embody the character and capacities of the institution.

3. Consider the advantages of evolutionary—rather than revolutionary—curricular change.

4. Scrutinize programs relying solely on distribution requirements to achieve general education goals.

5. Focus above all on the needs of students.

6. Empower a dedicated committee, not a standing one, with responsibility for curricular change.

7. Ensure adequate support for curricular change.

8. Understand that genuine curricular reform typically requires more than one year—not several months.

9. Create new forums for the discussion of progress on curricular reform.

10. Develop and sustain adequate constituency support for the committee's efforts.

11. Consider rolling out a reform plan in stages, rather than releasing a single final report.

12. While remaining realistic, don't allow environmental issues such as budget concerns to undermine the commitment to curricular discussion.

13. Engage students in curricular reform.

14. Avoid becoming mired in disagreements over the definition of terms; reach a working consensus and move on.

15. While encouraging a breadth of knowledge, recall that intellectual skills and the ability to integrate and apply knowledge are also critical.

16. In addition to important cognitive outcomes, be aware that general education often aspires to convey affective qualities, such as attitudes, values, and skills.

17. Remember that the cocurriculum makes an important contribution to students' general education.

18. Value the contribution all faculty members make—whatever their discipline or level of instruction—to supporting the institution's general education goals.

19. Acknowledge general education goals that are priorities of professional accrediting associations.

20. Do not assume that students will achieve unaided the integration of the disciplines they study; create a program that embodies integration.

21. Recognize that most change must come about through trade-offs rather than expansion.

22. Expand the campus debate by invoking an academy-wide discussion of general education.

23. Engage all important educational providers in the curricular discussion.

24. Be skeptical of curricular proposals that rest on faculty memories of their own student experience.

25. Awareness of how students learn can be as critical as determining what students are to learn.

26. Verify impressions with regard to experiences and views of relevant constituencies.

27. Be alert for changing circumstances and adapt planning strategies to address them.

28. Don't let searching for the "one best" program block incremental progress toward realistic reform.

29. Secure political support for any curricular proposal.

30. Avoid jargon that may alienate colleagues and others.

31. Engage actively in the debate and approval process.

32. Know the risks of introducing a curricular proposal in an open hearing.

33. If possible, disaggregate a complex proposal so that it may be considered in stages.

34. Seek the counsel of those who oppose the proposal.

35. Assume pragmatically that opponents are rational and operating in good faith.

36. Be sensitive to the legitimate fears of those who will be most affected by the curricular reform.

37. So far as possible, ensure broad understanding of the curricular proposal.

38. Do not rely solely on the academy's trust in logical argument to produce a positive decision.

39. Consider seeking approval through alternate means rather than through a business-as-usual process.

40. Agree to a definitive vote only when you are assured of a favorable outcome.

41. Do not assume that a negative vote is final; rather, make it clear that this will not be the case.

42. Beware of hijacking! Do not allow curricular reform to become a surrogate for some other issue.

43. Consider the advantages of some continuity between the planning team and the implementation process.

44. Include a staffing plan as part of a curricular reform proposal.

45. Make faculty and course development explicit priorities.

46. Endeavor to align the reward structure with the priorities of general education.

47. Seek to align the instructional requirements of new courses with faculty competencies.

48. Consider the advantages in the incremental implementation of a new program.

49. Assume that the implementation of any significant reform may reveal misalignments, gaps, and other limitations of the plan. Hence, consider initiating implementation through a trial run or pilot program.

50. Embed a commitment to productive assessment within the fiber of the program.

Appendix B
The Essential Learning Outcomes

Beginning in school, and continuing at successively higher levels across their college studies, students should prepare for twenty-first-century challenges by gaining:

Knowledge of Human Cultures and the Physical and Natural World

- Through study in the sciences and mathematics, social sciences, humanities, histories, languages, and the arts

Focused *by engagement with big questions, both contemporary and enduring*

Intellectual and Practical Skills, including

- Inquiry and analysis
- Critical and creative thinking
- Written and oral communication
- Quantitative literacy
- Information literacy
- Teamwork and problem solving

Practiced extensively, *across the curriculum, in the context of progressively more challenging problems, projects, and standards for performance*

Personal and Social Responsibility, including

- Civic knowledge and engagement—local and global
- Intercultural knowledge and competence
- Ethical reasoning and action
- Foundations and skills for lifelong learning

Anchored *through active involvement with diverse communities and real-world challenges*

Integrative and Applied Learning, including

- Synthesis and advanced accomplishment across general and specialized studies

Demonstrated *through the application of knowledge, skills, and responsibilities to new settings and complex problems*

Source: *College Learning for the New Global Century* (2007)

Note: This listing was developed through a multiyear dialogue with hundreds of colleges and universities about needed goals for student learning; analysis of a long series of recommendations and reports from the business community; and analysis of the accreditation requirements for engineering, business, nursing, and teacher education. The findings are documented in previous publications of the Association of American Colleges and Universities: *Greater Expectations: A New Vision for Learning as a Nation Goes to College* (2002), *Taking Responsibility for the Quality of the Baccalaureate Degree* (2004), and *Liberal Education Outcomes: A Preliminary Report on Achievement in College* (2005).

References

AACSB International. 2007. Eligibility procedures and accreditation standards for business accreditation. Tampa, FL: AACSB International.

ABET. 2007. *Criteria for accrediting engineering programs.* Baltimore, MD: ABET.

Association of American Colleges. 1985. *Integrity of the college curriculum: A report to the academic community.* Washington, DC: Association of American Colleges.

Association of American Colleges and Universities. 2004. *Taking responsibility for the quality of the baccalaureate degree.* Washington, DC: Association of American Colleges and Universities.

———. 2007. *College learning for the new global century: A report from the National Leadership Council for Liberal Education and America's Promise.* Washington, DC: Association of American Colleges and Universities.

———. 2008. *College learning for the new global century: Executive summary with employers' views on learning outcomes and assessment approaches.* Washington, DC: Association of American Colleges and Universities.

Astin, A. W. 1999. Student involvement: A developmental theory for higher education. *Journal of College Student Development* 40 (5): 518–29.

Awbrey, S. 2005. General education reform as organizational change: The importance of integrating cultural and structural change. *Journal of General Education* 54 (1): 1–21.

Bolman, L. G., and T. E. Deal. 1991. *Reframing organizations: Artistry, choice, and leadership.* San Francisco: Jossey-Bass.

Bok, D. 2006. *Our underachieving colleges.* Princeton, NJ: Princeton University Press.

Boyer, E. 1990. *Scholarship reconsidered.* New York: Carnegie Foundation for the Advancement of Teaching.

Boyer, E. L., and M. Kaplan. 1977. *Educating for survival.* New Rochelle, NY: Change Magazine Press.

Carnegie Foundation for the Advancement of Teaching. 1977. *Missions of the college curriculum.* San Francisco: Jossey-Bass.

Chandler, J. 1996. General education reform proposal runs into delays. @csun.edu 1 (8). www.csun.edu/~hfoao102/@csun.edu/csun96_97/csun1125_96/features/gened.html.

Chen, P. D., R. Gonyea, and G. Kuh. 2008. Learning at a distance: Engaged or not? *Innovate* 4 (3). www.innovateonline.info/index.php?view=article&id=438.

Task Force on the Core Curriculum. 1977. Harvard College: Cambridge, MA.

Council of Independent Colleges. 2003. Elmhurst hosts CIC liberal arts and business symposium. *Independent* (Fall).

Council on Undergraduate Research. About CUR. www.cur.org/about.html.

Eaton, J. S. 2008. Attending to student learning. *Change* 40 (4): 22–27.

Eastern Michigan University. Why general education? www.emich.edu/gened/whyGenEd.html.

Edgerton, R., K. O'Meara, and R. E. Rice, eds. 2005. *Faculty priorities reconsidered: Rewarding multiple forms of scholarship.* San Francisco: Jossey-Bass.

Ferris State University. Assessment Plan. www.ferris.edu/HTMLS/academics/gened/assess.html.

Flynn, W. J. 2005. The search for the learning-centered college. In *Establishing and sustaining learning-centered community colleges,* ed. C. J. McPhail, 1–12. Washington, DC: American Association of Community Colleges.

Gaff, J. G. 1980. Avoiding the potholes: Strategies for reforming general education. *Educational Record* 61 (4): 50–59.

———. 1981. Reconstructing general education: Lessons from Project GEM. *Change* 13 (6): 52–58.

———. 2003. Keep general education vital: A struggle against original sin? *Peer Review* 5 (4): 31.

Gardiner, L. F. 2000. Faculty development in higher education. The National Academy for Academic Leadership. www.thenationalacademy.org/readings/facdev.html.

Glassick, C. E., M. T. Huber, and G. I. Maeroff. 1997. *Scholarship assessed: Evaluation of the professoriate.* San Francisco: Jossey-Bass.

Hefferlin, J. B. 1969. Dynamics of academic reform. San Francisco: Jossey-Bass.

Huber, M. T., P. Hutchings, and R. Gale. 2005. Integrative learning for liberal education. *Peer Review* 7 (3–4): 4–7.

Knapp, L.G., J. E. Kelly-Reid, R. W. Whitmore, and E. Miller. 2007. *Employees in postsecondary institutions, fall 2005, and salaries of full-time instructional faculty, 2005–06.* Washington, DC: National Center for Education Statistics.

Levine, A. 1978. *Handbook on undergraduate curriculum.* San Francisco: Jossey-Bass.

Lindquist, Jack. 1996. Strategies for change. In *Handbook of the undergraduate curriculum: A comprehensive guide to purposes, structures, practices, and change,* eds. J. G. Gaff, J. L. Ratcliff, and Associates, 633–46. San Francisco: Jossey-Bass.

Lowell, A. L. 1938. *What a university president has learned.* New York: Macmillan.

Meacham, J. 2001. Faculty and students at the center: Faculty development for general education courses. *The Journal of General Education* 50 (4): 254–69.

Melusky, J. A., and D. M. Menis. 1996. Taking connections seriously: The new and improved SFC general education program. Paper presented at the conference of the Association for General and Liberal Studies, Daytona Beach, FL.

Miami Dade College. Learning outcomes at MDC. www.mdc.edu/learningoutcomes.

Miller, R. 2001. Use of part time faculty in higher education: Numbers and impact. www.greaterexpectations. org/briefing_papers/parttimefaculty.html.

Rice, R. E. 1991. The new American scholar: Scholarship and the purposes of the university. *Metropolitan Universities* 1 (4): 7–18.

Potashnik, M., and J. Capper. 1998. Distance education: Growth and diversity. *Finance and Development* 35 (1): 42–45.

Schmitz, B. 1992. *Core curriculum and cultural pluralism.* Washington, DC: Association of American Colleges.

Southern Illinois University Edwardsville. Baccalaureate reform through integrated design of general education. www.siue.edu/UGOV/FACULTY/BRIDGE.htm.

Southern Methodist University. Summary of general education experience. www.smu.edu/gened.

St. Cloud State University. Progress report on general education. www.stcloudstate.edu/generaleducation/story.asp?pubID=61&issueID=16440&storyID=21062

State University of New York at Buffalo. 1978. Application of the general education committee to the Project on General Education Models.

Steele, S. 2006. Curricular wars. *Journal of General Education* 55 (3–4): 161–85.

Task Force on the Core Curriculum, Harvard College. 1978. *Report on the core curriculum.* Cambridge, MA: Harvard University Press.

Task Group on General Education. 1988. *A new vitality in general education: Planning, teaching, and supporting effective liberal learning.* Washington, DC: Association of American Colleges.

University of Colorado at Boulder. Service learning. www.colorado.edu/servicelearning.

University of Oregon. The purpose of general education at the University of Oregon. www.uoregon.edu/~ustudies/US_Pages/US_GenEdu.html.

White, C. R. 1994. A model for comprehensive reform in general education: Portland State University. *Journal of General Education* 43 (3): 168–237.

About the Authors

Paul L. Gaston is trustees professor at Kent State University, where he was provost from 1999 to 2007. He earned the PhD and MA in English from the University of Virginia, where he was a Woodrow Wilson Fellow and a DuPont Fellow. He is the author of two books and has written extensively on subjects ranging from interart analogies, the poetry of George Herbert, and the fiction of Walker Percy, to academic strategic planning, the Higher Education Act, and the assessment of educational outcomes. Gaston has served on the faculty of the AAC&U Institute on General Education since 2001.

Jerry G. Gaff is senior scholar at AAC&U, where for thirty-three years, since 1975, he has worked for general and liberal education. He has been on the faculty of five institutions and served as a dean and university president. He has conducted research, directed national projects, published numerous books and articles, and consulted with scores of campuses to assure that students receive a broad liberal education. He has received many honors, including the Association for General and Liberal Education offering its faculty award in his name to recognize campus leadership for general and liberal education. Gaff has served on the staff of the AAC&U Institute on General Education since its inception.